THE MaGIC OF you

a COLORFUL BOOK OF HAPPINESS

LauRa Jane Jones

Published by Familius LLC, www.familius.com
PO box 1249 Reedley, Ca 93654

Familius books are available at special discounts for bulk purchases,
whether for sales promotions or for family or corporate use.
For more information, email orders@familius.com.

Library of Congress Control Number: 2021933760

Print ISBN 9781641704694

Printed in China

Edited by Lacey Wulf
Cover art and book design by Laura Jane Jones

10 9 8 7 6 5 4 3 2

First Edition

THE MaGIC of you

a COLORFUL BOOK of HAPPiNeSS

laura Jane Jones

INTRODUCTION

I believe that imagination is the closest thing to real magic that we have here on earth; what starts as a spark of inspiration can be imagined into a dream, and, if you really believe in that dream enough, you can find a way to turn what was once just an idea into something real.

This book is proof of that for me.

When I was a little girl, I had a dream, a secret dream that I didn't tell anyone else. This dream was born during trips to the school library and visits to bookshops, where I would pull books off the shelves in awe of their covers and colors. I imagined and dreamed that one day I would have a book on those shelves. However, I never said this dream out loud because I didn't think it would make sense to anyone else, other than me; I wasn't what you would call an avid reader or even a very passionate writer, but I loved books with color and pictures, or stories and poems that, even if they didn't have pictures, were full of color and magic. I was the kind of child who could be found sketching more than caught with her nose in a book at any spare moment, but I thought books were beautiful, just as they were, and there was something so exciting about picking out a new one.

So, I held that secret dream close to my heart, and the more I imagined it, the more it felt real. I had no idea how I would achieve it, but I just believed that someday I would do or accomplish something that would be interesting to enough people to turn it into a book. I carried that dream with me as I grew up; I went to university, studied education, fell in love with children's books all over

again, and though my life went in a direction so unrelated to that secret dream, I still believed in it.

Then I went to work, and I found it hard. Going out into the "real world" is challenging on us dreamers because everything becomes about practicality, logic, and making realistic choices. I felt the weight of the real working world crush so many of my dreams, and I reverted back to my safe space . . . my imagination.

In my imagination, the harsh everyday realities could be overcome with creativity, and so I started to create. I learned photography, I built a blog, and over the course of time, I found my way back to one of my oldest of my childhood joys: drawing.

I drew what I felt; I illustrated my thoughts into words, and I shared them online, and the most wonderful, yet unexpected thing happened—people liked and connected with my art. Over time, the thing I had used as an escape from reality stepped out of my imagination and became something very real and very important to me and others. Then one day, the magic happened: someone thought that what I was doing was interesting to enough people that it could make a great book.

When I started putting this book together, I thought about what kind of book little Laura would have been drawn to pull off a bookshelf, and what messages teenager Laura would have appreciated seeing written on the pages. So, I created a book filled with messages and reminders to myself, and all of you, that what starts as a spark of imagination can grow into a dream, and if you let yourself trust in that dream, you can create something real from it. I created a book that I hope is as beautiful to look at as the messages it holds.

So if you don't think that being a dreamer is a grown-up thing to do or that the

hings you dreamed of doing as a child
hould be left in your childhood, remem-
ber that this book you are holding right
now would never have existed had I let
that secret dream go. I hope these little
messages will help you to trust yourself
and reconnect with dreaming. I hope
you will look for inspiration in the world
around you and begin to let yourself
learn and grow from it. Most of all, I
hope that you will hold onto your secret
dreams and believe that you can create
something wonderful from them.

laura
x x x

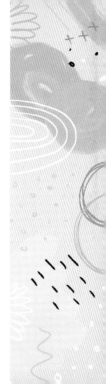

For all the Dreamers.

But also for Gio— the Dreamer who never lets me give up on mine.

LoVe

Our journey begins with
selfless self-love.

Self-Love starts with embracing who you are...

Self Love

IS NOT SELFISH

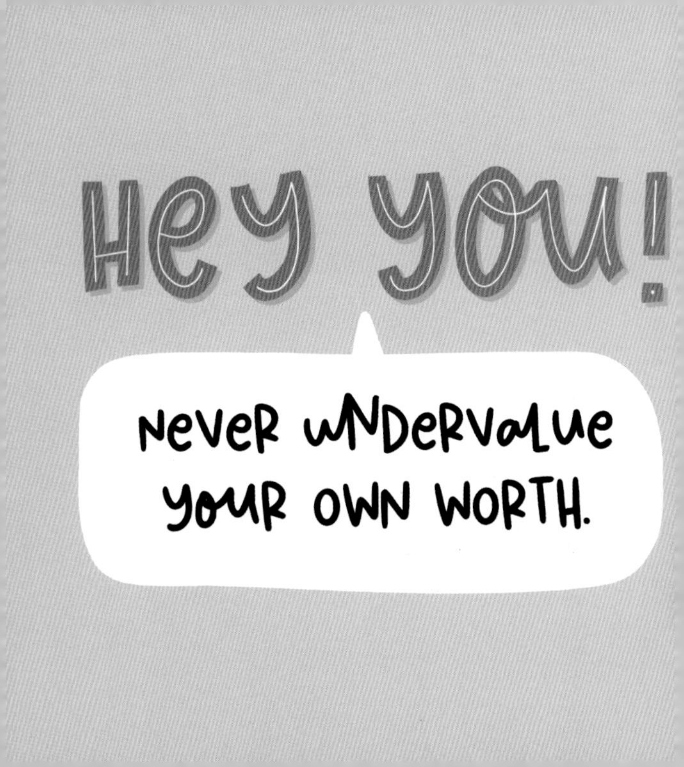
HEY YOU!
NEVER UNDERVALUE YOUR OWN WORTH.

The UNIVERSE LoveS
You & NeeDS You
To LeaRN To Love
YouRSelf

I HOPE
You KNOW
HOW LOVED
You aRe

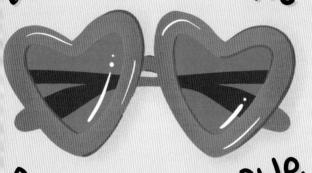

DON'T LET ANYONE

DIM YOUR SPARKLE

you are equally worthy of the love you give out so freely

IT'S NEVER TOO LATE TO CHOOSE TO MEND THAT RELATIONSHIP WITH YOURSELF. START TODAY.

Make The
RelaTionSHiP
You Have
WiTH YourSelf
a PRiority

REMEMBER:

- [ ] Self-acceptance
- [ ] Self-belief
- [ ] Self-forgiveness
- [ ] Self-care
- [ ] Self-confidence
- [ ] Self-love

IT'S OKAY TO SET
BOUNDARIES & MAKE
SPACE FOR WORKING ON
YOURSELF. THERE IS NO
SHAME IN PRIORITIZING
ME TIME.

self-RESPECT &...

SELF WORTH

SELF-LOVE FIRST

WE ARE MADE FROM LOVE TO BE LOVED.
WHEN YOU LEARN TO LOVE YOURSELF FIRST, EVERYTHING ELSE WILL FALL INTO PLACE...

Self-Care Day Recipe

1. ON A LARGE COUCH, COMBINE ONE PAIR FLUFFY SOCKS WITH ONE SET OF COMFY PAJAMAS.

2. ROLL IN ONE COZY BLANKET, ADDING A PILLOW IF DESIRED.

3. ADD TWO TO THREE CUPS HOT TEA WITH BISCUITS OR CHOCOLATE AND SIMMER UNTIL CHILLED.

4. GARNISH WITH POSITIVE MANTRAS, DEEP CALMING BREATHS, AND FURRY FRIEND CUDDLES.

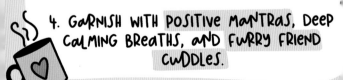

PROMISE TO
ACCEPT &
LOVE YOURSELF
AS YOU ARE,
FLAWS & ALL.

LiFe IS TOO SHORT
TO Be anyTHING
OTHeR THAN COMPLeTeLy
& UNaPOLOGeTiCaLLy
you.

HEY YOU!

YOU ARE WORTHY &
DESERVING OF YOUR
OWN LOVE.

The Ten Self-Love Commitments

1. Be fearless in the pursuit of what sets your soul on fire.
2. Trust in the universe & that it will guide you where you need to go.
3. Refuse to let yourself be boxed in or held back by labels.
4. Trust your gut.
5. Follow your heart.
6. Be open to change & the lessons found in every challenge.
7. Be responsible for your own happiness.
8. Accept & embrace all your feelings.
9. Celebrate your imperfections.
10. Be fully & unapologetically you.

DReaM

Don't let doubt or fear stand in the way of imagination & dreams.

IF YOU CAN DREAM IT...

YOU CAN DO IT

YOUR ONLY
LIMIT
IS WHAT YOU
CAN IMAGINE.

NEVER LET SOMEONE ELSE'S OPINION OF YOUR DREAMS STOP YOU FROM FOLLOWING THEM.

every GReaT
accomPLISHMenT
Once StaRTeD
aS a DReaM...

NoTe To SeLF:

DON'T GIVe uP
ON YOUR
DReaMS

YOU'RE NEVER
TOO OLD TO
USE YOUR
IMAGINATION

NOTE TO SELF:

DON'T LET THE
FEAR OF FAILURE
STOP YOU FROM
DREAMING.

DON'T LET
FeaR STOP YOU
FROM FOLLOWING
YOUR DReaMS

I DReaM MY
BeST DReaMS
WHeN I'M
WIDe awake

YOUR POTENTIAL
IS LIMITLESS

GROWING UP
DOESN'T MEAN
YOU HAVE TO
GIVE UP
DREAMING

IMAGINATION IS THE CLOSEST THING WE HAVE TO REAL MAGIC

SOMEDAY YOU'LL
TELL OF HOW
IT ALL STARTED
WITH HOPE &
DREAMS

JUST IMAGINE
THE POSSIBILITIES
YOU HAVEN'T
EVEN DREAMED
OF YET.

DON'T BE afRAID TO DReaM BIG

SomeDay
all The Things
You DReaM &
IMaGINe CoulD Be
YouR ReaLiTY

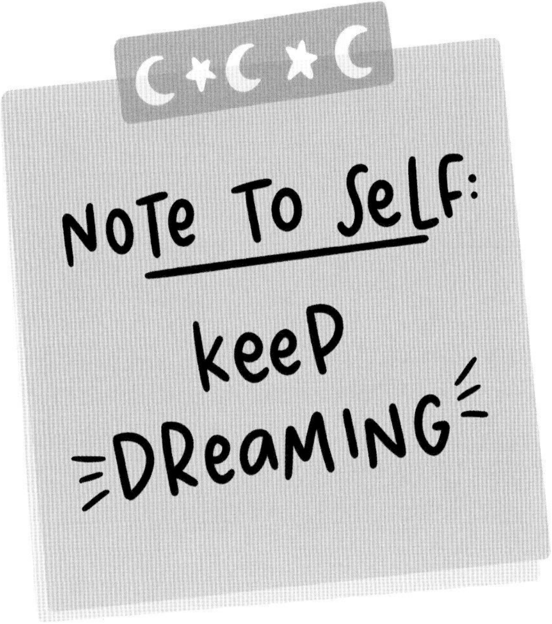
NOTE TO SELF:
KEEP
DREAMING

IMAGINE
HOW DIFFERENT
THE WORLD WOULD
BE IF THE DREAMERS
OF THE PAST HAD
GIVEN UP ON
THEIR DREAMS

BELIEVE

There is magic in you; you
just have to believe in it to
set it free.

WHEN you Believe
IN yourSelf
THe POSSIBILITIES OF
WHaT you caN DO
aRe LIMITLeSS.

LET GO OF
DOUBT IT'S
HOLDING YOU
BACK

BELIEVE IN WHO
YOU ARE &
WHAT YOU WANT;
BELIEVE IN THE
ABILITIES WITHIN YOU
TO DO GREAT THINGS

You're stronger than that voice in your head telling you "you can't"!

LET SELF-BELIEF
BE YOUR
≋SUPERPOWER≋

THINK OF WHAT
you could achieve
IF you LET GO
OF all DOUBT &
JUST Believe.

YOU LIGHT
UP WHEN YOU
BELIEVE IN
YOUR DREAMS

YOU DON'T HAVE TO FEEL BRAVE TO DO BRAVE THINGS.

NOTE TO SELF:

YOU CAN DO
HARD THINGS!

SOMEDAY
YOU'LL LOOK BACK
AT THIS MOMENT
& BE GLAD YOU
TOOK THAT
CHANCE

THE MOST
WONDERFUL
THINGS aRE
Waiting FOR
you

FAILURE IS NOT
THE ENEMY OF
SUCCESS,
SELF-DOUBT IS.

aMaZING THINGS
CaN HaPPeN
WHeN you CHOOSe
To BeLIeVe
IN THe MaGIC
THaT IS you

Believe you are

WORTHY

OF GREAT THINGS

Be YOUR OWN
CHeeRLeaDeR
ON THe HaRD Days

Repeat
after me:
I am a
self-believer.

HOLD ON TO HOPe & let IT LIGHT uP your DaRKEST Days...

GROW

Embrace the constant
changes of life & learn to
grow through them.

a MISTAKE ONLY
BECOMES a LOSS
IF we Fail TO See HOW
we CaN GROW FROM
WHaT IT TauGHT uS.

GROW aT YOUR OWN PaCE
IN YOUR OWN WaY

GROWTH IS NOT a LINEAR PROCESS; THERE WILL BE UPS, DOWNS & EVERYTHING IN BETWEEN.

GROWTH MINDSET

& DEEP BREATHS

BLOCK

I LIKE THINGS AS THEY ARE RIGHT NOW. I DON'T WANT THEM TO CHANGE.

GROWTH

CHANGE IS NECESSARY FOR GROWTH & I AM READY TO GROW.

DON'T COMPARE
YOUR PROGRESS
TO THAT OF THOSE
AROUND YOU

Be PRESENT
IN THE PROCESS

CHANGE IS
THE ONLY
CONSTANT;
EMBRACE
IT FULLY.

BE PATIENT YOU'RE STILL LEARNING

IT WON'T HAPPEN
all aT once, BUT
SOMEDay you'll
Look Back &
See HOW FaR
you've come...

BLOCK

I DON'T WANT TO TRY BECAUSE I'M AFRAID OF MAKING A MISTAKE

GROWTH

I KNOW THAT THE MISTAKES I MAKE WILL HELP ME LEARN & IMPROVE

THINK OF ALL THE
THINGS YOU'VE ALREADY
GROWN THROUGH, ALL
YOU'VE LEARNED &
HOW YOU'VE CHANGED...
YOU MADE IT THROUGH
SO MUCH, NOW
KEEP GOING.

We Need Both The Rainy Days & The Sunny Days To Grow, Bloom & Thrive.

Be Brave,
Like the little
seed that pushes
through the dark
to reach the
sunlight.

I AM NOT
afraID TO GROW
THROUGH CHANGE

BLOCK

I've TRIED THIS BEFORE & I WASN'T ANY GOOD AT IT.

GROWTH

IF I NEVER TRY AGAIN, I'LL NEVER LEARN WHAT I AM REALLY CAPABLE OF.

FORGIVE YOURSELF

everyone makes MISTakes.
everyone MESSES uP FROM
Time To Time.
LET GO OF THE PaST &
Move FORWARD
WITH GOOD INTENTIONS.

WHAT IF I FAIL?

BUT, WHAT IF YOU SUCCEED?

CREATE

Find your creative flow
& create from a place
of pure joy.

you create
your own
happiness

ACTION IS WHAT TURNS DREAMS INTO REALITY

THE FLOWERS
DON'T WAIT FOR
PERMISSION TO
BLOOM &
NEITHER SHOULD
you

YOU ARE
THE DESIGNER
& CREATOR
OF YOUR OWN
FUTURE

CReaTe
FROM a Place
OF Joy

WHEN you CREATE FROM a PLACE OF INSPIRATION, YOU WILL FIND YOUR FLOW

CREATION IS a PROCESS. Make SPACE FOR THE exPERIENCE.

YOU DON'T HAVE TO KNOW THE DESTINATION TO BEGIN THE ADVENTURE

CReaTe,
IF ONLY
BeCaUSe IT
MakeS youR
LIFe MoRe
JoyFuL

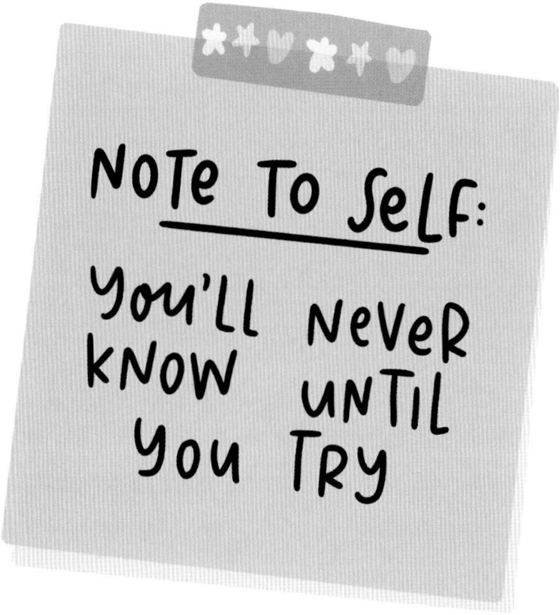
NOTE TO SELF:
YOU'LL NEVER KNOW UNTIL YOU TRY

CLOSE YOUR
EYES &
OPEN YOUR MIND
TO ALL THE IDEAS
JUST WAITING
TO BE BROUGHT
TO LIFE

CReaTe
THe LiFe
You'Ve
IMaGINeD

CREATIVITY
IS HOW WE
CHANGE IDEAS
INTO REALITIES

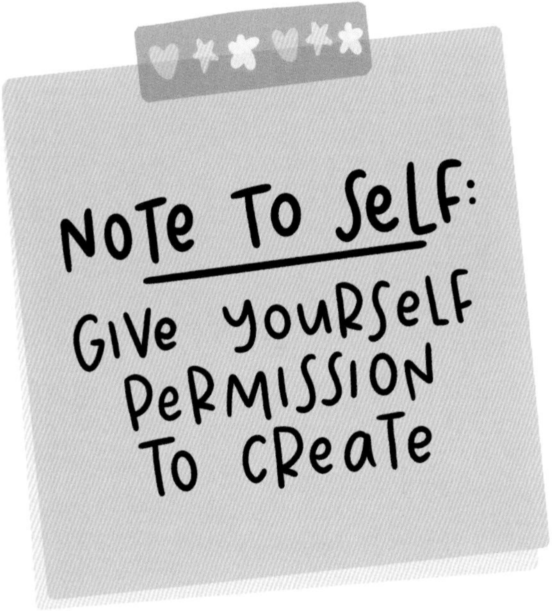
NOTE TO SELF:
GIVE YOURSELF PERMISSION TO CREATE

CREATE FOR
PERSONAL JOY,
NOT FOR
EXTERNAL
VALIDATION

CREATE YOUR DREAMS

CREATE YOUR DREAMS

CREATE YOUR DREAMS

CREATE YOUR DREAMS

DON'T CHASE YOUR DREAMS-
CREATE THEM.

TO CREATE
SOMETHING
FROM NOTHING
IS PROOF OF
THE MAGIC
THAT IS YOU...

THERE IS MAGIC IN
you & WHEN you
CREATE FROM A PLACE
OF JOY, IT FLOWS OUT
THROUGH you AND
MAKES THE WORLD A
LITTLE BIT BETTER
THAN IT WAS BEFORE
you STARTED.

aBouT THE auTHOR

Laura Jane Jones is the illustrator and creator behind @laurajaneillustrations on Instagram, where she uses her art to open up conversations around mental health, feminism, environmental awareness, and more. Laura is passionate about making social media a more positive and safe space, and to use the impact of social reach to spread awareness about important topics.

aBout Familius

Visit Our Website: www.familius.com

Familius is a global trade publishing company that publishes books and other
tent to help families behappy. We believe that the family is the fundamental u
of society and that happy families are the foundationof a happy life. We recog
that every family looks different, and we passionately believe in helping allfam
find greater joy. To that end, we publish books for children and adults that inv
families to live the Familius Ten Habits of Happy Family Life: love together, p
together, learn together, work together, talktogether, heal together, read toge
eat together, laugh together, and give together. Founded in 2012, Familius
located in Sanger, California.

Connect

Facebook: www.facebook.com/familiustalk

Twitter: @familiustalk, @paterfamilius1

Pinterest: www.pinterest.com/familius

Instagram: @familiustalk

"The most important work you ever do will be within the walls of your own ho